BARN QUILT BLANKETS

Sarah Thompson

rich textures
CROCHET

RichTexturesCrochet.com

Table of Contents

RichTexturesCrochet.com

INTRODUCTION

Learn to crochet five beautiful barn quilt blankets

The tradition of barn quilts is thought to have begun hundreds of years ago. Colourful designs were painted onto the sides of barns to help identify them and the families who lived there. In many rural communities, these colourful designs still decorate the countryside.

This collection of blanket crochet patterns was inspired by these colourful designs and aims to bring the tradition and comfort of what they represent into your home.

In the following pages, you will discover five beautiful crochet patterns including a barn quilt blanket for each season. Each crochet pattern is easy to work and crafted in a worsted/medium weight yarn.

It is my hope that these crochet blankets will inspire and bring warmth to your home and the homes of the people you love and care for.

Happy Crocheting!

Sarah Thompson

MATERIALS AND TOOLS

Yarn:

Each of the crochet patterns in this book was completed using worsted/medium weight (4) yarn called Heartland by Lion Brand Yarn.

Heartland is a soft, 100% acrylic yarn that is available in a variety of earth-tone colours. Exact amounts and colours will be given at the start of each pattern.

You may, however, use your favourite worsted weight yarn for this project. You may also use a favourite yarn fibre, although I do recommend a yarn type that is durable and easy to wash.

Hook:

For these crochet patterns, you will need a 5 mm (H/8) crochet hook. You may change the size of your crochet hook as needed to obtain the correct gauge.

Remember, if you make any changes to the yarn or hook, you may also need to adjust the amount of yarn used in each project.

Notions:

Along with your yarn and hook it may be helpful to have a pair of scissors, yarn needle, and measuring tape on hand. Supplies for blocking your completed blanket are optional.

BASIC SQUARE PATTERN

Each of the blankets in this pattern book is created by working 64 blanket squares and then crocheting them together. Each square is approximately 6 x 6 inches and constructed using the same stitch pattern. All that changes to create the image in the blanket is the colour.

The crochet pattern that follows is the basic blanket square. For each blanket, you will make 64 of these squares either in a single colour or in two colours. To know what colour to make the squares and other particular details for each design, turn to the particular blanket pattern.

SKILL LEVEL: EASY

GAUGE: 20 STITCHES X 20 ROWS OF MOSS STITCH PATTERN = 4 INCHES

INDIVIDUAL SQUARE FINISHED SIZE: 6 X 6 INCHES

YARN: HEARTLAND BY LION BRAND YARN (100% EXTRA ACRYLIC; 5 OZ/142G; 251 YDS/230 M) OR A WORSTED/MEDIUM WEIGHT YARN OF YOUR CHOICE.

EACH BLANKET SQUARE REQUIRES APPROXIMATELY 41 YARDS OF YARN.

HOOK: SIZE H/8 (5 MM) HOOK.

NOTIONS: YARN NEEDLE.

Notes: This crochet pattern is written using American crochet terms. Each square is worked corner to corner in rows. Turn at the end of each row. Weave in your ends as needed.

Ch 2.

Row 1: Work 3 sc into the 2nd ch from your hook. Ch 2, turn. (3 sc)

Row 2: Sc in the 1st st, ch 1, sk the next st, 2 sc in the next st. Ch 2, turn. (3 sc)

Row 3: Sc in the 1st st, ch 1, sk the next st, sc in the next ch-1 sp, ch 1, sk the next st, 2 sc in the final ch-2 sp. Ch 2, turn. (4 sc)

Row 4: Sc in the 1st st, [ch 1, sk the next st, sc in the next ch-1 sp] twice, ch 1, sk the next st, 2 sc in the final ch-2 sp. Ch 2, turn. (5 sc)

Row 5: Sc in the 1st st, [ch 1, sk the next st, sc in the next ch-1 sp] three times, ch 1, sk the next st, 2 sc in the final ch-2 sp. Ch 2, turn. (6 sc)

Row 6: Sc in the 1st st, [ch 1, sk the next st, sc in the next ch-1 sp] four times, ch 1, sk the next st, 2 sc in the final ch-2 sp. Ch 2, turn. (7 sc)

Row 7: Sc in the 1st st, [ch 1, sk the next st, sc in the next ch-1 sp] five times, ch 1, sk the next st, 2 sc in the final ch-2 sp. Ch 2, turn. (8 sc)

Continued...

Row 8: Sc in the 1st st, [ch 1, sk the next st, sc in the next ch-1 sp] six times, ch 1, sk the next st, 2 sc in the final ch-2 sp. Ch 2, turn. (9 sc)

Row 9: Sc in the 1st st, [ch 1, sk the next st, sc in the next ch-1 sp] seven times, ch 1, sk the next st, 2 sc in the final ch-2 sp. Ch 2, turn. (10 sc)

Row 10: Sc in the 1st st, [ch 1, sk the next st, sc in the next ch-1 sp] eight times, ch 1, sk the next st, 2 sc in the final ch-2 sp. Ch 2, turn. 11 sc)

Row 11: Sc in the 1st st, [ch 1, sk the next st, sc in the next ch-1 sp] nine times, ch 1, sk the next st, 2 sc in the final ch-2 sp. Ch 2, turn. (12 sc)

Row 12: Sc in the 1st st, [ch 1, sk the next st, sc in the next ch-1 sp] 10 times, ch 1, sk the next st, 2 sc in the final ch-2 sp. Ch 2, turn. (13 sc)

Row 13: Sc in the 1st st, [ch 1, sk the next st, sc in the next ch-1 sp] 11 times, ch 1, sk the next st, 2 sc in the final ch-2 sp. Ch 2, turn. (14 sc)

Row 14: Sc in the 1st st, [ch 1, sk the next st, sc in the next ch-1 sp] 12 times, ch 1, sk the next st, 2 sc in the final ch-2 sp. Ch 2, turn. (15 sc)

Row 15: Sc in the 1st st, [ch 1, sk the next st, sc in the next ch-1 sp] 13 times, ch 1, sk the next st, 2 sc in the final ch-2 sp. Ch 2, turn. (16 sc)

Row 16: Sc in the 1st st, [ch 1, sk the next st, sc in the next ch-1 sp] 14 times, ch 1, sk the next st, 2 sc in the final ch-2 sp. Ch 2, turn. (17 sc)

Row 17: Sc in the 1st st, [ch 1, sk the next st, sc in the next ch-1 sp] 15 times, ch 1, sk the next st, 2 sc in the final ch-2 sp. Ch 2, turn. (18 sc)

Row 18: Sc in the 1st st, [ch 1, sk the next st, sc in the next ch-1 sp] 16 times, ch 1, sk the next st, 2 sc in the final ch-2 sp. Ch 2, turn. (19 sc)

Row 19: Sc in the 1st st, [ch 1, sk the next st, sc in the next ch-1 sp] 17 times, ch 1, sk the next st, 2 sc in the final ch-2 sp. Ch 2, turn. (20 sc)

Row 20: Sc in the 1st st, [ch 1, sk the next st, sc in the next ch-1 sp] 18 times, ch 1, sk the next st, 2 sc in the final ch-2 sp. Ch 2, turn. (21 sc)

NOTE: If changing colours, switch to colour B at the end of row 20. Fasten off colour A. Complete rows 21-40 in colour B.

TO CHANGE COLOURS: In the final sc of row 20, with colour A, insert your hook in the final sp, yo and draw up a loop. Drop colour A, pick up colour B and draw it through the 2 loops on your hook. Fasten off colour A. With colour B, ch 2, turn.

Row 21: Sc in the 1st st, [ch 1, sk the next st, sc in the next ch-1 sp] 18 times, ch 1, sk the next st, sc2tog inserting your hook into the final ch-1 sp and ch-2 sp. Ch 2, turn. (19 sc, 1 sc2tog)

Row 22: Sk the 1st st, sc in the ch-1 sp, [ch 1, sk the next st, sc in the next ch-1 sp] 17 times, ch 1, sk the next st, sc2tog inserting your hook into the final ch-1 sp and ch-2 sp. Ch 2, turn. (18 sc, 1 sc2tog)

Row 23: Sk the 1st st, sc in the ch-1 sp, [ch 1, sk the next st, sc in the next ch-1 sp] 16 times, ch 1, sk the next st, sc2tog inserting your hook into the final ch-1 sp and ch-2 sp. Ch 2, turn. (17 sc, 1 sc2tog)

Row 24: Sk the 1st st, sc in the ch-1 sp, [ch 1, sk the next st, sc in the next ch-1 sp] 15 times, ch 1, sk the next st, sc2tog inserting your hook into the final ch-1 sp and ch-2 sp. Ch 2, turn. (16 sc, 1 sc2tog)

Row 25: Sk the 1st st, sc in the ch-1 sp, [ch 1, sk the next st, sc in the next ch-1 sp] 14 times, ch 1, sk the next st, sc2tog inserting your hook into the final ch-1 sp and ch-2 sp. Ch 2, turn. (15 sc, 1 sc2tog)

Row 26: Sk the 1st st, sc in the ch-1 sp, [ch 1, sk the next st, sc in the next ch-1 sp] 13 times, ch 1, sk the next st, sc2tog inserting your hook into the final ch-1 sp and ch-2 sp. Ch 2, turn. (14 sc, 1 sc2tog)

Row 27: Sk the 1st st, sc in the ch-1 sp, [ch 1, sk the next st, sc in the next ch-1 sp] 12 times, ch 1, sk the next st, sc2tog inserting your hook into the final ch-1 sp and ch-2 sp. Ch 2, turn. (13 sc, 1 sc2tog)

Row 28: Sk the 1st st, sc in the ch-1 sp, [ch 1, sk the next st, sc in the next ch-1 sp] 11 times, ch 1, sk the next st, sc2tog inserting your hook into the final ch-1 sp and ch-2 sp. Ch 2, turn. (12 sc, 1 sc2tog)

Row 29: Sk the 1st st, sc in the ch-1 sp, [ch 1, sk the next st, sc in the next ch-1 sp] 10 times, ch 1, sk the next st, sc2tog inserting your hook into the final ch-1 sp. Ch 2, turn. (11 sc, 1 sc2tog).

Row 30: Sk the 1st st, sc in the ch-1 sp, [ch 1, sk the next st, sc in the next ch-1 sp] 9 times, ch 1, sk the next st, sc2tog inserting your hook into the final ch-1 sp and ch-2 sp. Ch 2, turn. (10 sc, 1 sc2tog)

Row 31: Sk the 1st st, sc in the ch-1 sp, [ch 1, sk the next st, sc in the next ch-1 sp] 8 times, ch 1, sk the next st, sc2tog inserting your hook into the final ch-1 sp and ch-2 sp. Ch 2, turn. (9 sc, 1 sc2tog)

Row 32: Sk the 1st st, sc in the ch-1 sp, [ch 1, sk the next st, sc in the next ch-1 sp] 7 times, ch 1, sk the next st, sc2tog inserting your hook into the final ch-1 sp and ch-2 sp. Ch 2, turn. (8 sc, 1 sc2tog)

Row 33: Sk the 1st st, sc in the ch-1 sp, [ch 1, sk the next st, sc in the next ch-1 sp] 6 times, ch 1, sk the next st, sc2tog inserting your hook into the final ch-1 sp and ch-2 sp. Ch 2, turn. (7 sc, 1 sc2tog)

Row 34: Sk the 1st st, sc in the ch-1 sp, [ch 1, sk the next st, sc in the next ch-1 sp] 5 times, ch 1, sk the next st, sc2tog inserting your hook into the final ch-1 sp and ch-2 sp. Ch 2, turn. (6 sc, 1 sc2tog)

Row 35: Sk the 1st st, sc in the ch-1 sp, [ch 1, sk the next st, sc in the next ch-1 sp] 4 times, ch 1, sk the next st, sc2tog inserting your hook into the final ch-1 sp and ch-2 sp. Ch 2, turn. (5 sc, 1 sc2tog)

Row 36: Sk the 1st st, sc in the ch-1 sp, [ch 1, sk the next st, sc in the next ch-1 sp] 3 times, ch 1, sk the next st, sc2tog inserting your hook into the final ch-1 sp and ch-2 sp. Ch 2, turn. (4 sc, 1 sc2tog)

Row 37: Sk the 1st st, sc in the ch-1 sp, [ch 1, sk the next st, sc in the next ch-1 sp] twice, ch 1, sk the next st, sc2tog inserting your hook into the final ch-1 sp and ch-2 sp. Ch 2, turn. (3 sc, 1 sc2tog)

Row 38: Sk the 1st st, sc in the ch-1 sp, ch 1, sk the next st, sc in the next ch-1 sp, ch 1, sk the next st, sc2tog inserting your hook into the final ch-1 sp and ch-2 sp. Ch 2, turn. (2 sc, 1 sc2tog)

Row 39: Sk the 1st st, sc in the 1st ch-1 sp, ch 1, sk the next st, sc2tog inserting your hook into the final ch-1 sp and ch-2 sp. Ch 2, turn. (1 sc, 1 sc2tog)

Row 40: Sk the 1st st, sc2tog inserting your hook into the final ch-1 sp and ch-2 sp. (1 sc2tog)

Fasten off and weave in your ends.

Now that you know how to make the basic blanket square, continue to your favourite blanket pattern and complete the squares in the colours required for that project. You are then ready to join your squares together.

HOW TO JOIN YOUR SQUARES TOGETHER

Lay your squares out in a grid design using the colour charts as a guide that are available at the end of each blanket edging instruction.

There are many ways to join blanket squares. I like to join them with a row of single crochet stitches.

When joining your squares together, use a piece of yarn that is the same colour as at least one of the blanket squares that you are joining.

With the right side facing (so that you work your single crochet stitches on the front side of your blanket), join your yarn with a sl st at one end of the square row.

Working through both thicknesses (the square above and below), work a row of single crochet stitches across the seam, inserting your hook through the lower square and then the square above it, crocheting the two squares together. Across each square, I worked 20 single crochet stitches. You may work any number of stitches, however you will want to work the same number of stitches across each square to ensure the joins are even.

At the end of the square, simply jump to the next two squares, pulling the yarn a little tighter between the stitches to pull the two squares together.

I worked my horizontal rows first and then the vertical rows. Change your yarn colour as needed as you work your way across the blanket.

At the end of the row, fasten off and weave in your ends. Repeat for all rows and columns.

Materials

Yarn:

3060 yards total of a worsted/medium weight yarn including:

- 750 yards dark blue (includes amounts to work the edging)
- 660 yards of white
- 660 yards of light blue
- 330 yards of black
- 660 yards of grey

Finished Measurements:

51 x 51 inches

Squares Needed

Referring to the Basic Square Pattern on page 5, make a total of 64 squares in the following colours:

4 squares in dark blue

4 squares in white

4 squares in light blue

8 squares in black/light blue

8 squares in grey/light blue

8 squares in white/light blue

16 squares in white/grey

4 squares in grey/black

4 squares in grey/dark blue

4 squares in black/dark blue

Wintertime Barn Quilt

Easy / Facile / Fácil

Once you have completed all of your blanket squares, you will join them together using the following colour chart as a guide. For instructions on joining your squares together, refer to page 11.

Notes:
- Edging of the blanket is worked in rounds.
- Edging of the blanket may be worked in any colour of your choosing. In the pictures shown here I have worked the edging in my darkest blue.
- Join at the end of each round, do not turn.

WINTERTIME BARN QUILT EDGING

Join yarn with a sl st in the 1st st of any side and proceed as follows:

Rnd 1: Ch 1, *[evenly work 19 hdc across the first blanket square, hdc in the top of the next seam] 7 times, evenly work 19 hdc across the final blanket square of that side, 1 hdc in the corner**, turn blanket so that you are working along the next side; Rpt from * around your blanket ending the final repeat at ** when you come to the 1st st. Join with a sl st in the top of the 1st st. Do not turn. (640 sts)

Rnd 2: Ch 1, fpdc around the post of the 1st st, *[bpdc around the post of the next st, fpdc around the post of the next st] across until you come to the next corner st, [bpdc, fpdc, bpdc] around the post of the corner st; Rpt from * around until you come to the 1st st. Join with a sl st in the top of the 1st st. (648 sts)

Rnd 3: Ch 1, fpdc around the post of the 1st st, bpdc around the post of the next st, *[fpdc around the post of the next st, bpdc around the post of the next st] across until you come to the next corner st, [fpdc, bpdc, fpdc] around the post of the corner st; Rpt from * around until you come to your final st, bpdc in the final st. Join with a sl st in the top of the 1st st. (656 sts)

Rnd 4: Ch 1, fpdc around the post of the 1st st, *[bpdc around the post of the next st, fpdc around the post of the next st] across until you come to the next corner st, [bpdc, fpdc, bpdc] around the post of the corner st; Rpt from * around until you come to the final 2 sts, fpdc around the post of the next st, bpdc around the post of the next st. Join with a sl st in the top of the 1st st. (664 sts)

Fasten off, weave in your ends and block if desired.

Materials

Yarn:

2920 yards total of a worsted/medium weight yarn including:

- 600 yards purple (includes amounts to work the edging)
- 1150 yards of white
- 250 yards of dark green
- 250 yards of light green
- 170 yards of dark pink
- 330 yards of light pink
- 170 yards of yellow

Finished Measurements:

51 x 51 inches

Squares Needed

Referring to the Basic Square Pattern on page 5, make a total of 64 squares in the following colours:

4 squares in purple

16 squares in white

8 squares in purple/white

8 squares in dark green/light green

4 squares in light green/white

8 squares in white/light pink

4 squares in white/dark green

4 squares in yellow/dark pink

4 squares in dark pink/light pink

4 squares in yellow/light pink

Tulip Barn Quilt

Easy / Facile / Fácil

Once you have completed all of your blanket squares, you will join them together using the following colour chart as a guide. For instructions on joining your squares together, refer to page 11.

Notes:
- Edging of the blanket is worked in rounds.
- Edging of the blanket may be worked in any colour of your choosing. In the pictures shown here I have worked the edging in purple.
- Join at the end of each round, do not turn.

TULIP BARN QUILT EDGING

Join yarn with a sl st in the 1st st of any side and proceed as follows:

Rnd 1: Ch 1, *[evenly work 19 hdc across the first blanket square, hdc in the top of the next seam] 7 times, evenly work 19 hdc across the final blanket square of that side, 1 hdc in the corner**, turn blanket so that you are working along the next side; Rpt from * around your blanket ending the final repeat at ** when you come to the 1st st. Join with a sl st in the top of the 1st st. Do not turn. (640 sts)

Rnd 2: Ch 1, sc in the 1st st and in each st around working 3 sc in each corner st. Join with a sl st in the 1st st. (648 sts)

Rnd 3: Ch 1, CL in the same st as joining, *ch 1, sk the next st, [CL in the next st, Ch 1, sk the next st] across to the next corner st, [CL, ch 2, CL] in the next corner st; Rpt from * around. Join with a sl st in the top of the 1st st. (328 CL sts)

Rnd 4: Ch 1, sc in the top of each CL st and in each ch-1 sp around working 3 sc in each ch-2 corner sp. Join with a sl st in the top of the 1st st. (664 sts)

Rnd 5: Ch 1, hdc in each st around working 3 hdc in each corner st. Join with a sl st in the 1st st. (672 sts)

Fasten off, weave in your ends and block if desired.

Special Stitch: CL ([yarn over, insert your hook into the indicated st, yarn over and draw up a loop, yarn over and draw through 2 loops] three times, yarn over and draw through all the loops on your hook. Cluster Stitch made.

Materials

Yarn:

2975 yards total of a worsted/medium weight yarn including:

- 500 yards dark green (includes amounts to work the edging)
- 165 yards of light green
- 250 yards of brown
- 250 yards of orange
- 1150 yards of yellow
- 660 yards of white

Finished Measurements:

51 x 51 inches

Squares Needed

Referring to the Basic Square Pattern on page 5, make a total of 64 squares in the following colours:

4 squares in brown
8 squares in white
4 squares in light green/white
8 squares in yellow/white
16 squares in yellow
4 squares in dark green/white
4 squares in light green/yellow
4 squares in dark green/yellow
8 squares in yellow/orange
4 squares in orange/brown

Sunflower Barn Quilt

Easy / Facile / Fácil

Once you have completed all of your blanket squares, you will join them together using the following colour chart as a guide. For instructions on joining your squares together, refer to page 11.

Notes:
- Edging of the blanket is worked in rounds.
- Edging of the blanket may be worked in any colour of your choosing. In the pictures shown here I have worked the edging in dark green.
- Join at the end of each round, do not turn.

SUNFLOWER BARN QUILT EDGING

Join yarn with a sl st in the 1st st of any side and proceed as follows:

Rnd 1: Ch 1, *[evenly work 19 hdc across the first blanket square, hdc in the top of the next seam] 7 times, evenly work 19 hdc across the final blanket square of that side, 1 hdc in the corner**, turn blanket so that you are working along the next side; Rpt from * around your blanket ending the final repeat at ** when you come to the 1st st. Join with a sl st in the top of the 1st st. Do not turn. (640 sts)

Rnd 2: Ch 1, sc in the 1st st and in each st around working 3 sc in each corner st. Join with a sl st in the 1st st. (648 sts)

Rnd 3: Ch 1, cone st in the 1st st and in each st around, working 3 cone sts in each corner st. Join with a sl st in the 1st st. (656 sts)

Rnd 4: Ch 1, sc in the 1st st and in each st around working 3 sc in each corner st. Join with a sl st in the top of the 1st st. (664 sts)

Fasten off, weave in your ends and block if desired.

Special Stitch: Cone St (Insert your hook in the next st, yo and draw up a loop, yo and insert your hook in the space UNDER the same stitch just worked, yo and draw up a loop, yo and draw through all the loops on your hook. Cone Stitch made.)

Materials

Yarn:

2505 yards total of a worsted/medium weight yarn including:

- 785 yards red (includes amounts to work the edging)
- 85 yards of light green
- 125 yards of dark green
- 105 yards of brown
- 45 yards of black
- 45 yards of yellow
- 1315 yards of white

Finished Measurements:

51 x 51 inches

Squares Needed

Referring to the Basic Square Pattern on page 5, make a total of 64 squares in the following colours:

25 squares in white

13 squares in red

9 squares in white/red

2 squares in light green/white

2 squares in yellow/white

2 squares in black/red

6 squares in dark green/white

5 squares in brown/white

Cardinal Barn Quilt

Easy / Facile / Fácil

Once you have completed all of your blanket squares, you will join them together using the following colour chart as a guide. For instructions on joining your squares together, refer to page 11.

Notes:
- Edging of the blanket is worked in rounds.
- Edging of the blanket may be worked in any colour of your choosing. In the pictures shown here I have worked the edging in red.
- Join at the end of each round, do not turn.

CARDINAL BARN QUILT EDGING

Join yarn with a sl st in the 1st st of any side and proceed as follows:

Rnd 1: Ch 1, *[evenly work 19 hdc across the first blanket square, hdc in the top of the next seam] 7 times, evenly work 19 hdc across the final blanket square of that side, 1 hdc in the corner**, turn blanket so that you are working along the next side; Rpt from * around your blanket ending the final repeat at ** when you come to the 1st st. Join with a sl st in the top of the 1st st. Do not turn. (640 sts)

Rnd 2: Ch 1, sc in the 1st st and in each st around working 3 sc in each corner st. Join with a sl st in the 1st st. Turn. (648 sts)

Rnd 3: Ch 1, bobble in the 1st st, *sc in the next st, 3 sc in the next (corner) st, sc in the next st, bobble in the next st, [sc in each of the next 3 sts, bobble in the next st] across to the next corner; Rpt from * around ending with an sc in each of the final 3 sts. Join with a sl st in the 1st st. (656 sts)

Rnd 4: Ch 1, sc in the 1st st and in each st around working 3 sc in each corner st. Join with a sl st in the top of the 1st st. (664 sts)

Fasten off, weave in your ends and block if desired.

Special Stitch: Bobble St ([yarn over, insert your hook into the indicated st, yarn over the draw up a loop, yarn over and draw through 2 loops] 5 times, yo and draw through all the loops on your hook. Bobble Stitch made.)

Poinsettia Barn Quilt

Materials

Yarn:

2885 yards total of a worsted/medium weight yarn including:

- 910 yards red (includes amounts to work the edging)
- 410 yards of light green
- 250 yards of Dark Green
- 165 yards of black
- 165 yards of yellow
- 985 yards of white

Finished Measurements:

52 x 52 inches

Squares Needed

Referring to the Basic Square Pattern on page 5, make a total of 64 squares in the following colours:

16 squares in white

8 squares in red

8 squares in white/red

8 squares in light green/white

4 squares in yellow/red

4 squares in yellow/black

4 squares in black/red

12 squares in dark green/light green

Easy / Facile / Fácil

Once you have completed all of your blanket squares, you will join them together using the following colour chart as a guide. For instructions on joining your squares together, refer to page 11.

Notes:

- Edging of the blanket is worked in rounds.
- Edging of the blanket may be worked in any colour of your choosing. In the pictures shown here I have worked the edging in red.
- Join at the end of each round, do not turn.

POINSETTIA BARN QUILT EDGING

Join yarn with a sl st in the 1st st of any side and proceed as follows:

Rnd 1: Ch 1, *[evenly work 19 hdc across the first blanket square, hdc in the top of the next seam] 7 times, evenly work 19 hdc across the final blanket square of that side, 1 hdc in the corner**, turn blanket so that you are working along the next side; Rpt from * around your blanket ending the final repeat at ** when you come to the 1st st. Join with a sl st in the top of the 1st st. Do not turn. (640 sts)

Rnds 2-6: Ch 1, working in the 3rd loop all the way around, hdc in the 1st st and in each st around working 3 hdc in each corner st. Join with a sl st in the 1st st. (648/656/664/672/680 sts)

Fasten off, weave in your ends and block if desired.

Special Stitch: 3rd Loop - Looking at the back of your hdc st you will see a horizontal bar/loop running along under the back loop of the stitch. This is called the "3rd loop."

Abbreviation Chart

ABBREVIATION	DESCRIPTION
BPDC	BACK POST DOUBLE CROCHET
CH	CHAIN STITCH
CH-SP	CHAIN SPACE
DC	DOUBLE CROCHET
FPDC	FRONT POST DOUBLE CROCHET
HDC	HALF DOUBLE CROCHET
RPT	REPEAT
SC	SINGLE CROCHET
SC2TOG	SINGLE CROCHET TWO STITCHES TOGETHER
SK	SKIP
SL ST	SLIP STITCH
SP	SPACE
ST	STITCH
STS	STITCHES
YO	YARN OVER
*	REPEAT THE INSTRUCTIONS FOLLOWING THE SINGLE ASTERISK AS DIRECTED

US to UK Stitch Conversion

US TERM	UK TERM
CHAIN (CH)	CHAIN (CH)
SLIP STITCH (SL ST)	SLIP STITCH (SL ST)
SINGLE CROCHET (SC)	DOUBLE CROCHET (DC)
SINGLE CROCHET TWO TOGETHER (SC2TOG)	DOUBLE CROCHET TWO TOGETHER (DC2TOG)
HALF DOUBLE CROCHET (HDC)	HALF TREBLE (HTR)
DOUBLE CROCHET (DC)	TREBLE (TR)
HALF TREBLE (HTR)	HALF DOUBLE TREBLE (HDTR)
TREBLE/TRIPLE (TR)	DOUBLE TREBLE (DTR)

Yarn Weight Conversion Chart

US TERM	UK TERM	AU TERM	SYMBOL
JUMBO	ROVING	20 PLY	7 JUMBO
SUPER BULKY	SUPER CHUNKY	16 PLY	6 SUPER BULKY
BULKY	CHUNKY	12 PLY	5 BULKY
WORSTED WEIGHT	ARAN	10 PLY	4 MEDIUM
LIGHT WORSTED	DK (DOUBLE KNITTING)	8 PLY	3 LIGHT
SPORT WEIGHT	SPORT WEIGHT	5 PLY	2 FINE
FINGERING OR SOCK WEIGHT	4 PLY OR SOCK WEIGHT	4 PLY OR SOCK WEIGHT	1 SUPER FINE
FINGERING OR SOCK WEIGHT	3 PLY OR BABY	3 PLY	1 SUPER FINE
LACE WEIGHT	2 PLY OR LACE WEIGHT	1-3 PLY	0 LACE

Crochet Hook Conversion Chart

MILLIMETER SIZE	US SIZE
2.25mm	B/1
2.5mm	--
2.75mm	C/2
3mm	D
3.25 mm	D/3
3.5mm	E/4
3.75mm	F/5
4mm	G/6
4.5mm	7
5mm	H/8
5.5mm	I/9
6mm	J/10
6.5mm	K/10.5
7mm	--
8mm	L/11
10mm	N/P/15
15mm	P/Q

Notes

About the author

Sarah Thompson has been designing crochet patterns since 2018. It wasn't until 2020 that she left her day job to design full-time. She works under the name Rich Textures Crochet, where her original crochet patterns focus on the beauty of textured stitches. She continues to inspire many in the art of crochet. She lives in Ontario, Canada, with her husband, their four children and two energetic dogs. Find her free crochet patterns at richtexturescrochet.com and video tutorials on YouTube @RichTexturesCrochet

Acknowledgements

Thank you to the following people who have been instrumental in the publishing of this book:

First and foremost, to my husband, Andrew, and my children for all of your love and support. You challenge me daily to step out of my comfort zone. I love to see the looks of excitement (and sometimes confusion) on your faces when I show you my latest design. You are my greatest encouragers and I love you!

Thank you to my Dad, Glen, and mom, Debbie, now passed, for your love, and for always encouraging me in my creativity and teaching me to take risks. I love you!

To Mona, who sat patiently with me that one summer, teaching me the basics of crochet and helping me crochet my first little lace bell: Thank you!

To Magi, friend and author. Thank you for your patience and detail in answering all of my book publishing questions. You are an inspiration!

Thank you to Brittany at One Busy B Photography for capturing beautiful portraits of my blankets. I appreciate your creativity and artistic eye!

And finally, thank YOU, fellow creator and artist, for taking the time to enjoy and work through my crochet patterns. Your love for crochet and the beautiful creations that you share with me are inspiring!

Happy Crocheting!

Sarah Thompson